As She Blooms

Alicia kaylee peat

BookLeaf Publishing
India | USA | UK

Made with ❤ on the BookLeaf Publishing Platform
www.bookleafpub.in
www.bookleafpub.com

Dedication

To all the women who taught me self love

Preface

Acknowledgements

1. The healing

I am fond of you
fond of the weary nights moonlight conversation
memory of your pain a numbness lingers on my skin
reminisce, sad songs, sing along in the background of
bad days like a comfort of a warm blanket,
synchronizing melodies to my hearts agony
i am fond of you
underneath these new blueprint's of my skin are still the
scars of you
I am fond of your reflection eyes that look into mine
I see her.
I hear her.
I will remember her as I am her.
fond of a past, though will no longer define me releasing
the hurt
this is the healing

2. The garden

She was a sunflower amongst roses
In a garden of every flower
as roses bloom, bold, beautiful unapologetically
mothered from the same soil, she grew
A sunflower rising to the sun. All she wanted was to reach the moon.
flowers showered by the rain storms petals fall as petals do
A sunflower, amongst roses and flowers, she watched as they still bloomed seasons came seasons, go she wanted to be a rose or how she envied the beauty the first pick to a bouquet beautifully arranged. She was a sunflower delicate.
she wish she was brave as a dandelion
Sweet as honeysuckles
Elegant like daisies
Peaceful like lavender
she was a sunflower
but the sun loved her so
She's the sun's special flower

she's what makes summer days
She's the smile on a rainy day
Not a rose
Not a daisy
Nor honeysuckle or lavender
shes among the flowers in a garden
The flowers in the garden
Beautiful as designed

3. Hard too love

were flowers to much of an ask
nor diamond rings upon my hand
id rather rocks an shells if it kept you forever
id settle for whenever
no love letters my Romeo no Shakespeare
you're no poet as I yearn to hear you say I love you in a million different ways
to choose me amongst the wonders of the seven seas, a fisherman that only fish for me
nor gold or rubies more valuable than loyalty
no man made money no status of royalties. A woman with no need of lavish only gift me with beautiful memories. Buy me the things the heart may value no need for your dimes and nickels.
is my asking too big of you?
has my heart ached for more than it can handle?
oh my was the weight of my love too much to hold.
Should I shed the pounds shrink myself down empty my cup until I am digestible enough?

darling, then would I be worthy of love

4. In love with thy self

I buy the daisies sweet smell of femininity fills the room
fresh white linen on my body
skin to skin I trace the creation of the Gods with admiration
in the voids of silence a calming in the lonely
my companion is the sky an bees it's sweet
hummingbirds bring me melodies
radiance of inner peace no man shall disrupt my oasis
nor trespass my garden of Eden
forever daisies will bloom an shall all the flowers be as beautiful as I
coexisting amongst the beautiful creations
how delicate the pretty things are
so pure of heart
I shower in affirmations
relish in the blessings
to be of skin and bone
yet burden by a heavy soul
admirably so

to be in love with one's self is to know how to love someone else

5. Roses

Roses are bold
roses are delicate
delivered with love
delivered with loss
age with grace as petals will fray
divine beauty
a rose knows it's value
for thorns shall shed blood of thy who lust with greed of
its beauty
a rose of many shades
passion of red
pink an feminine
the innocence of white
friendships of yellow
courageous black
in a garden of art shall roses bloom
my darling rose
bloom

6. Her death

Do not mourn her
shes no longer here
do not ask of her last words
when you dismissed of her voice
Do not mourn her
you shall not linger for her sweet lips
it wasn't her you kissed
do not mourn her
shes not here
mourn the way she loved before
bury the love letters
your promises left unkept
bury the deafening sound of her begging to be loved by
you
bury all she was to you
Do not mourn her
the funeral is for you

7. Rebirth

unfamiliar skin untouched unharmed
sweet sent in the air unaware I can breath
this is air this is life
To have a heart with a steady beat
soothing like melody
no longer rushing waves of anxiety
tranquility in my body
this unfamiliar void filled with something like a kind of jubilation
my mind in a deep meditation
this is me without dread
or feeling quite dead
Alive as if I've never lived life jaded
never walked along a straight line falling over hopes and dreams
This Is me with aspirations
Chasing figments of my imagination
this is healing
this is hoping
finally coping

8. Shoulder for you

Lay here heavy head lay weary
Lay down your thoughts what has you disheartened
heavy eyes hold seas of tears
Rest assured on my shoulders
bare weight of your sorrows
for a better tomorrow
No burden to big
mines to take yours to give
may hands rest upon your shoulder
for I be your placeholder
cry out your seas I'll swim
dig your grave I'll unearth the soils
have no fear mercy is the lord
I am his soldier he gave me strength for I am your shoulder
lean on me

9. Goodbye

When love feels like a strain
walk towards faith
when bruises don't mend
fend
when words cut deep hold the pen
confess sins of sinner
if there is war
your worth fighting for
when your hearts on the line
walk a change in direction
A path of redirection
introspection
when love feels like rejection
remember love is affection
when love cheats
Dont be defeat owe your self loyalty
You heart is worth royalties
when love calls back
and it will call back

leave a message at the tone
Goodbye

10. Dear younger self

When your tears fill a ocean learn how to swim
When the boys give you flowers
Don't deflower your petals for lust
Know who you can trust
When heart break consumes you
Fill the void with faith
Don't mistake your liquor for a cure
Never change your heart so pure
When the pain can no longer endure
Let love humble you
But never would love fumble you
Stay true to the heart the world will tear you apart
When your at the end remember where you start
Not everything that ends deserves to mend
Remember the devil was once a friend
Scars are battles of the mind
All wars end in due time
In your journey it's yourself you must find

11. It’s okay

Being broken is okay
you don't have to smile today
Put the mask away
your playing pretend but im no longer ten don't read me
lines full of lies saying your fine
behind the scenes let me pull curtains please
being broken is okay
Don’t suffocate screams
Don’t hold back tears and swallow your fear
Stop checking under the bed the monsters are in head
Being broken is okay
Don’t hide the scars
Your truth is in all the beautiful imperfect parts
Your art
Being broken is okay
Don’t leave just stay
An just say
I’m broken an it’s okay
It’s only for today

Being broken is okay
One day I'll be okay

12. The wrecking

shes no need of rescue her chamber is in her mind these
chains that hold her aren't seen with eyes
He sees her
Her caged heart he's a wrecking ball trying to tear her
walls apart
Some walls protect you others shield you from the things
you need most
Who knew love was a wrecking ball
Who knew love is what she needed most

13. The Woman

The earth
The birth of kings an queens
The creators divine design
The boldness of storms the calmness of rain
The depth of the ocean her uncharted body
The mind of a galaxy secrets unknown
The eyes of daggers piercing souls
The heart of saffron
The soul of stars
The nature of wolves
The elegance of fine wine
The intelligence of ancient Gods
The woman

14. Beautiful insanity

She ran away deep in her mind to find herself
She lost herself within the maze of her mind
That was her beautiful insanity

15. Flowers an decay

Parts of me I mourn
I mourn how I laughed without conscience
Love fully without apprehension
Spoken
Without being silenced
Free spirit oh how fond of you I use to be
Bold eyes now of haze in shades of gray
Envy of a beating heart once mellowed drums an guitar
Now a sad violin
Of a one man, Orchestra
How I wish I could forget ya
Sweet as you were
Before your flower bloomed
Innocent child
Blossom as you may
How I mourn you
So full of a life
Unharmed
A virgin of worldly wrath's

Soft like nature
Oh so sweet so naïve you could be
Oh I envy the dead
Darling come back to me

16. New again

Forsaken sins u don't define me
My uncharted waters are seas I dive
Deep under water for unclaimed treasure
No purest form of riches then the love I found for myself
Unapologetically selfish
My value known nor shall it decrease
Breath
Air I claim I'm allowed to take up as much space
No confinement for my mind or heart
Shall my soul never part
For this faith keeps me afloat

17. Butterflies

Who knew butterflies were warning signs
flutters in my stomach
words stabbing at my throat
lady bugs are posion
roses an their thorns
how beautiful yet deceiving
shedding lies as a snake sheds it's skin
how promising a apple taste even when it's sin
love dressed as lust
just a moth attracted to the light oh how it bares
unaware it'll die
oh love a slient kill
oh how a butterfly drains your blood such a pretty thing
could cost you so much

18. I am

I am
Blooming bold big an bright
under
Luminous lustful light
Revengeful red rose
Unapologetically unhinged
Wild wishful
Intergalactic, intelligence
Extraterrestrial extraordinaire
i am
Summers smoke
under sunset silhouette
I am
Dark daring devious delight
the
Feminine fire furry
burning in my eyes
I am

19. Breath

Breath
just existing among the creations
breath
a voice amongst a crowded room
breath
a body in the ocean
a soul among the stars
breath
i can feel
breath
I can see
breath
I can live another day
thats alot more then some can say

20. Growth

You never truly stop growing
the leaves change as seasons do
leaves crumble beneath you
lovers come lovers go
loves that stay with you keeps close to home
you never truly stop growing
The grass turns green, then slowly decays underneath
roots grow deeper into the soil.
We never leave our roots.
We all have an end each one of us knows yet where our
story began.

21. A million ways to love yourself

keep the flowers near the window seal oh how admirable
they are compared to you
love notes signed an addressed
a box of chocolate sweet as you
oh how easy it is to love you
slip on the dress or even undress
mirror the art of you
sweet love songs sing so beautifully
sleep into a deep dream
relax
breath you are divine
limitless time
make loving your self worth wild

www.ingramcontent.com/pod-product-compliance
Lightning Source LLC
Chambersburg PA
CBHW051749130826
49812CB00033B/1076
* 9 7 8 9 3 7 0 9 2 7 8 6 5 *